M000215963

The Power of Management Innovation

"The pacesetters are the organizations that consistently, relentlessly, and successfully recognize, emphasize, and utilize competitively strong new ways of deploying and integrating their companies' total resources in new and more effective category-breaker ways to seize today's strong business opportunities."

"The early years of the 21st century have been an incubator of great opportunities for businesses that understand and respond to their new marketplaces and global requirements.

"Today's pacesetter companies do not view their strength in enabling growth in terms of the *quantity of management* of the hierarchical leadership of an earlier day."

The Power of Management Innovation

24 Keys for Sustaining and Accelerating Business Growth and Profitability

ARMAND V. FEIGENBAUM
President and CEO, General Systems Company

DONALD S. FEIGENBAUM
Executive Vice President and COO, General Systems Company

McGRAW-HILL
New York Chicago San Francisco Lisbon
London Madrid Mexico City Milan New Delhi
San Juan Seoul Singapore Sydney Toronto

1 2 3 4 5 6 7 8 9 0 DOC/DOC 3 2 1 0 9

ISBN-13: 978-0-07-162578-4
ISBN-10: 0-07-162578-X

McGraw-Hill books are available at special quantity discounts to use as premiums and sales promotions, or for use in corporate training programs. To contact a representative, please visit the Contact Us pages at www.mhprofessional.com.

Contents

The Power of Management Innovation

☑ The Power of Management Innovation

The opening years of the 21st century have provided great opportunities for companies that understand and respond to their new marketplaces and global requirements. These years have also shaken companies that have been slow to recognize and deal with the fundamental changes in the economic and social forces that have created these opportunities.

Many companies have continued to develop as powerful agents of business improvement. Some have declined in growth and profitability.

Two basic characteristics stand out in the companies that are most successful in leadership and management: their quality of management and what we call their *management capital.*

Quality of management involves the leadership passion, the populism, and the disciplined responsibility for sustaining and accelerating business growth and profitability, particularly in the following ways:

- Customer value leadership including product and service that's a lock on the future
- Operating cost leadership for a company's economic strength
- Empowering a company culture of superior performance

Management capital is a company's overarching theme for effectively recognizing, developing, accumulating, deploying, and measuring the capacity and effectiveness of its total resources—hard assets and soft assets—to achieve these results in sustaining and accelerating growth and profitability.

One of the primary characteristics of this new 21st-century management is its emphasis on *innovation*. This is characterized by the institutionalization, through infrastructure and integration, of constant *management innovation*, which is also a necessary condition for successful product and service research and development. The emphasis on successful business innovation in pacesetter companies positions those companies for further innovation.

These 24 keys are intended to convey the essentials and the importance of innovation in driving business success in the 21st century, as presented in our book, *The Power of Management Capital*. We wrote our book to express and recognize the modern field of management as a body of leadership, technological, behavioral, economic, and multinational knowledge. The application and value of modern management extend far beyond its origins in industrial business operations. Modern management is now also recognized as essential in organizational performance ranging from education, government, and medicine to international bodies and technology. And smart innovation leads to success in all of these areas.

Our emphasis is on the application of new ways to improve results in an enormously demanding and brutally competitive economic, social, political, and international environment.

The Power of Management Innovation is intended for the men and women who are responsible for the performance of their organizations, large and small—the people who can lead the drive for innovation.

"The opening years of the 21st century have been a shattering experience for companies that have been slow to recognize and deal with the fundamental changes in the economic and social demands but it has been a continuing opportunity for those organizations that make management innovation a foundation of their business."

☐ ~~Innovate now and then~~

☑ **Innovate constantly**

An important characteristic of a pacesetter company is that it emphasizes *management innovation* not as periodic events but as a general and constant theme, an ongoing process, a prevailing attitude. This orientation defines the organization. The company emphasizes innovation in order to increase its business value for customers and key stakeholders.

These are management innovations, such as lean production, robust product development, team organizations, just-in-time management, and quality management. The business leaders understand and believe in the nature of such innovation, management process improvement, and the human and teamwork commitment they require, and lead and encourage their development.

The force behind this innovation is what we have termed a company's *management capital*. This is a strategy for capitalizing the management power of a company's leaders to recognize, develop, accumulate, deploy, and measure the capacity of its total resources to sustain and accelerate its growth and profitability. Management innovation is central to this success.

An increasing and evolving emphasis on developing and implementing management capital is the root of success in sustaining growth.

Innovation has long been recognized as a principal determinant of economic growth. In recent years the importance of management innovation has become one of the most significant influences on economic performance.

Here are three lessons to learn from this experience:

Innovate: Understand the importance of the constancy of management innovation. What worked well in the past may not work now.

Learn from other companies: Know how your competitors are working any advantage. Understand how companies in other industries lead the others.

Avoid obsessing over an initiative: Realize the danger of becoming too fond of any business leadership initiative, no matter how popular. Be careful about not sticking with any one initiative for too long.

"One characteristic of pacesetter companies ... is their emphasis on the competitive power that results from making management innovation systematic ... while simultaneously also recognizing and preserving the competitive strength of their fundamental and unique signature capabilities."

☐ ~~Trust the old ways~~

☑ **Promote innovation**

One primary characteristic of the new management model—management capital—is how innovation is understood, appreciated, and emphasized. The focus is on the institutionalization of constant management innovation, integrated throughout the organization.

The reason for this is that a successful business innovation is not an end in itself. It also positions a company for the next innovation.

In every industry, from silicon and steel to optics and genetics, it is also a necessary condition for connecting systematic product R&D throughout the entire company—not only focusing it on a central research laboratory—and enhancing the assurance of its timing and success.

Some companies have not yet recognized this reality; they do not fully understand that they have been outclassed by competitors, in many cases because they have not understood this management model. Many of the companies that have worked with this model still have a way to go toward implementing it fully.

There are seven key areas of this new power of management capital for integrating resources, promoting innovation in all those resources, and increasing income through surpassing competitors:

1. Thorough understanding of the tectonic shift in the character of business investment in profit-driving assets and in the management model for using these assets to achieve strong results

2. Leadership with the passion, populism, and disciplined responsibility to exorcise old management doctrines and replace them with new and more powerful practices

3. Systematic identification of the key opportunities for aggressively using this new power of management capital

4. Clear identification and assurance of the effectiveness of the key management capital channels for delivering results, including digitization where appropriate

5. Full understanding of the management capital tools and measurements that can be used to achieve the best results

6. Effective management of capital structuring, recognizing the role of intangible assets

7. Consistent delivery of results for company stakeholders, emphasizing the principle that the company earns its income from customers, not the financial community

Here are three ways to promote innovation:

Understand the fundamentally new character of business innovation: Understand the potential for sharpening your competitive edge.

Expand innovation: Promote it not just in terms of products, but also to improve and ensure the institutionalization of R&D. Make it an overarching theme for your entire organization.

Develop management innovation: Make it constant. Integrate it throughout the organization.

"Pacesetter companies are generally quite aware of the fundamentally new character of business innovation. They consistently, relentlessly, and successfully develop competitively strong new ways of deploying and integrating their companies' total resources."

☐ ~~Stay the course~~

✔️ **Learn and innovate**

The effects of innovation have long been recognized as a principal determinant of economic growth. In recent years the importance of management innovation has become one of the principal factors in that determinant. While difficult to quantify and measure, its results are recognized as one of the most significant influences on economic performance.

In the 1980s, an era of increasing business leadership for Japan, the Nikkei 225 Index grew significantly. During that period, many American and other Western managers visited Japan to learn about "Japanese management." Innovative management in all its forms was clearly recognized as fundamental in powering Japan's increasing world leadership in industries ranging from automobiles to consumer electronics.

As those Japanese innovations became better known throughout the United States and the West, they spread across many companies, helping them build their business strength. Those imported innovations became powerful center points to add to the strong competitive improvement initiatives already under way in those organizations. Meanwhile, the pace of the leading-edge management innovation in Japan seemed to slow. The Nikkei 225 Index began to drop and continued to drop significantly, while increases in American and Western economic performance indicators reflected corresponding improvements in business results.

During the 1990s, American and other Western companies increasingly became the leaders in newer developments that became important keys to the resurgence of the American and Western business economies, even though many Japanese companies—from automobiles to electronics—maintained their customer quality leadership.

One important factor underlying this economic change is that long-term economic expansions create major business disconnects. In some companies, the relentless development of new areas of management leadership was not always institutionalized as the fundamental leading edge it had become.

Consider these three lessons on the importance of constancy of management innovation:

Remember that what rises can also fall: Innovation helped some companies rise. An inability to institutionalize the development of new areas of management caused some to begin to fall.

Learn from failures as well as from successes:
Learn from what companies have done right. Learn
from what companies have done wrong. Sometimes
it's only what they've failed to continue doing right.

Be attentive to business disconnects: Recognize
these problems that result from long-term economic
expansions. Innovation and growth are successes
only if you can sustain them.

**"One of the lessons of innovative experi-
ence is to avoid two of the biggest competitive
dangers—becoming too fond of any business
leadership initiative and sticking with an initiative for too long."**

☐ ~~Manage hard the old way~~

☑ Manage smart in new ways

Quality of management is central. Company leaders must systematically develop and integrate market and leadership capabilities, technology capacities, brand names, customer relationships, human resources, international connections, business processes, and supply networks.

Companies must consider these factors in terms of both physical assets and financial capital. It's critical to emphasize smart management of all resources—soft and hard—in a strong infrastructure and in connection with the "e-frastructure" of the Internet for productivity and e-commerce. The integration of total capacities is the key to sustaining profitability.

In the last several years there has been an increasing emphasis on the form, frequency, and scope of leadership for establishing superiority in the way a company works throughout all aspects of its organization and its customer, supplier, relationship, and alliance networks to establish a competitive advantage.

This leadership model includes promoting systematic integration with fundamentally based leading-edge management processes as a necessary condition for maximizing long-term business results from information technology. Relentless business and management innovation is a basic key to technology value creation. This key consists of leadership emphasis on the management principle that digitizing a flawed process only enables that flawed process to operate faster.

Information technology is a "general-purpose" technology. Like earlier transforming technologies such as electricity and radio, information technology is a foundation both for creating new products and services and for establishing new ways to manage them. Managing these technologies encourages and requires complementary organizational investments, such as new business processes and work practices.

In contrast to the earlier technologies, however, information and the Internet have increasingly changed the shape of 21st-century management and leadership itself.

This change has been demonstrated in the fast, fact-based, decision-making managerial support power of information technology and the faster-paced, less bureaucratic results provided in both intranet and Internet forms for self-organizational individual actions within a company's infrastructure.

Do these three things to manage smarter in new ways:

Emphasize quality of management: Measure it in terms of the know-how for focusing full resources on the new management and leadership models and a strong infrastructure. Take advantage of unusual growth opportunities. Resolve problems of significant business disconnects.

Lead smart: Succeed with passion, populism, and disciplined responsibility. Strive to understand and effectively manage total resources and relationships. Understand the new strength of business management innovation.

Go virtual: Develop the potential of e-commerce. Maximize use of the Internet for strong product growth and effective productivity growth.

"Their uses of hard assets and soft assets are the competitive strengths of pacesetters. ... The integration of total capacities is the key to sustaining profitability."

☐ ~~Manage as always~~

☑ **Promote manage-
ment capital**

From the brutally competitive economy of the opening years of the 21st century, two areas of corporate emphasis have emerged. The first is a fundamentally new character of business innovation. The second is a powerfully new focus on the carryover business issues from the expansive economy of the 1990s and the early 21st century.

One example of the new character of business innovation is a new, more effective, and fully integrated use of technology resources for broad company competitive leadership. This is very different from the self-contained islands of technology that characterized some organizations. Company technology is integrated across all product and service development and throughout all operations, marketing, and distribution areas as a fundamental competitive leadership strategy.

Another example of the new character of business innovation is the improving development and use of brand names and branding. When a company consistently develops and effectively coordinates the focus of its brands, the results align its character throughout the entire organization in powerful ways. It greatly improves recognition by customers and can significantly support sales.

These innovative actions to take advantage of opportunities bring into sharp focus the carryover business demands from the very different environment that characterized much of business during the 1990s and into the recent past. Throughout those years, companies expanded because of abundant resources, regulatory easing, strong technological growth, and acquisitions, mergers, and alliances. Customer demand and expectations were high and both customers and companies were willing to spend money to meet those expectations.

Business leadership is now characterized by depending less on very good markets or on single technological silver bullets. This type of leadership does not accept some past judgments that confused the results of a strong economy with assumptions about strong management practices.

Recognize these three lessons from recent problematic management practices:

__Emphasize achieving superior returns on financial capital invested in the business:__ This is a wiser course than focusing on short-term stock price increases. Go for growth, not greed.

***Avoid simply pursuing marketing trends with me-
too products and services:*** Don't market hot spots.
Develop products and services that provide greater
bottom-line advantages and longer-term customer
sales positioning.

Be cautious about mergers and acquisitions:
Make sure that the economic consequences do not
create balance sheet difficulties. Mergers and acquisitions should provide new competitive strengths and
new business value.

**"Pacesetting business leaders focus on
eliminating the resulting disconnects within
the company's management infrastructure and
on measuring and eliminating the business
failure costs that are their consequence."**

☑ The power of hard and soft assets

Opportunistic attitudes lead directly to further fundamental change in management in leading organizations. Managers are recognizing how the character of companies is changing.

The traditional concept of a company was largely based on hard assets and primarily hierarchical. This concept influenced the structuring of business in the United States and globally for several decades.

The new concept is that the business value of an organization resides in the way it combines the power of hard assets—finances, equipment, bricks and mortar—with the power of "soft" assets—productive, market, sales, human development factors. This combination includes such assets as these:

- Brand names and reputation for quality and customer satisfaction
- Technology, know-how, and patent rights
- Customer relationships and distribution arrangements

- Partnerships with suppliers and other business alliances
- International and global connections
- Capacity to attract and retain capable people and provide training and development
- International connections
- Sense of public responsibility
- Integration of technology, management, and human resources
- Responsibility of corporate governance

Companies have recognized this combination value in principle, and pacesetting companies are now applying that principle. It has become a fundamental focus in the way in which investment in companies has been changing, principally in understanding and managing business value.

Leaders now focus on value-added intangibles and soft assets as much as hard assets—and far more in some markets. This changes the meaning, skills, tools, and emphasis of management.

One of the primary characteristics of this new management model is how leaders understand and emphasize innovation. This is characterized by the institutionalization of constant management innovation, especially of intangibles, and integration of it into the infrastructure. The most significant characteristic of a successful business innovation is that it also positions a company for the next innovation—it is not just an end in itself.

Here are three ways to maximize on your soft assets:

Develop your business value: Recognize your combination of hard and soft assets. Build it, diffuse it, and network it.

Focus on value-added intangibles and soft assets: Understand that they are as important as hard assets, if not more. Change how you manage.

Institutionalize innovation: Integrate it into your infrastructure. Think of a successful innovation not just as an accomplishment but as positioning the company for more innovation.

"Annual investment in intangible 'soft' assets—research and development, advertising, software purchases, and so on—rose from 4 percent of the gross domestic product in 1978 to almost 10 percent in 2000, an enormous increase over two decades."

 ☐ ~~Grow through good markets~~

☑ Grow through opportunism

Systematizing management innovation has caused major changes that have affected the meaning and practice of leadership and management in pacesetter companies. More and more companies have been challenging (or at least redefining) the traditional top-down strategic and operational corporate approach— "We need a good market in order to grow vigorously." These companies have been pursuing new opportunities and developing new strategies. This is a major area of change among leading companies.

These opportunities are creating, expanding, and redefining markets for these companies and changing the ways they bring products and services to those markets. This opportunism opens a broad range of possibilities. For example:

- Using information technology to establish service markets for engineered and manufactured products
- Structuring e-commerce processes as a competitive advantage
- Pursuing a broad-scale partnership initiative for cooperation and alliances with companies that are competitors in some markets, creating close relationships that were once unthinkable

The attitude in pacesetter companies is bold and ambitious: "We'll develop the total competitive capability, both internally and through alliances, for marketizing these opportunities, to sustain profitable growth. We'll fully connect our total assets and resources for innovating the competitive strength to manage our way through whatever business conditions we must expect to face."

These companies also recognize that good markets will certainly help. However, they are not going to depend on the market alone. Instead, they are making their growth consistently opportunity-driven and long-term, which also makes them as "recession-proof" as possible.

Follow these three guidelines to grow through opportunism:

Do not depend on the market alone: Take advantage of good markets, of course, but don't trust them. Build your success and growth on opportunities.

Be opportunistic: Use information technology to develop service markets for your products. Make a competitive advantage out of your e-commerce processes. Form partnerships and alliances with other companies.

Learn from the leaders: Understand what leading companies accomplish. Don't imitate them unless you're sure what works for them will work for you. Instead, think about the reasons behind their changes, the ways in which opportunistic companies develop their strategies.

"An increasing number of companies have been moving toward a continuing emphasis on an entirely new spectrum of opportunities that are being created as New and Old Economies connect globally."

□ ~~Don't fix if it's not broken~~

☑ Keep aware and agile

Which factors have driven the strong growth of pacesetter companies in the United States and throughout the world? How can companies withstand slowdowns and major fluctuations that challenge long-term profitability?

How will these driving factors be influenced by the economic, social, and political churning and the brutally competitive global economy? How will the rapid gyrations in markets make it more difficult for .accounting practices to determine true performance costs and forecasting programs to establish the economic determinants of corporate planning?

As changes outside a business exceed productive changes within, it's more difficult for companies to thrive or even survive. Economic groundswells have overwhelmed many analytical and strategic approaches to evaluating and projecting company performance.

Decision making and action have become more complex for CEOs and management leaders in all markets and industries. This increased complexity has been changing the dimensions of business strategy and implementation, affecting a spectrum of issues, including the following:

- Investing in technology
- Leading real human resources initiatives
- Maintaining alliances successfully
- Determining the speed of new product or service development
- Setting time horizons for investments and financial planning
- Reducing production costs

Businesses are growing more intricate and at a faster speed. For example, consider the effects of venture capital financing, multiple marketing channel distribution, and new patterns of employee recruiting, development, and training. Product and service development initiatives must be more effective and faster; new offerings are being commoditized in months or even weeks, not years.

Growing demand for higher quality requires companies to become more effective, to improve the ways they manage customer relationships, and to develop supply chain processes. Quality audits will not guarantee customer loyalty. Basic business innovation must happen much faster.

These three warnings emerge from changes in the business environment:

Focus on fixed costs: Always a fundamental factor in managing profits and growth, fixed costs become even more important as variable costs decrease. When sales decline, reducing variable costs is generally less effective.

Be aware of the danger of maintaining high levels of development: It's a competitive necessity, but the corresponding high levels of fixed costs can accelerate cycles and fluctuations in profitability. Different approaches to innovation in management may be necessary.

Don't trust economies of scale: A company cannot maintain market dominance on volume alone. A dominant product may be displaced by the next temporarily dominant product. The basic premise of volume production is being challenged.

"This is a world where ... some of the founding principles, such as Adam Smith's 'invisible hand,' are being tested and reworked for the first time in more than 200 years."

☐ ~~Focus on profits~~

☑ Focus on customers

A consumer who is completely satisfied with a purchase tells six other potential buyers. A dissatisfied consumer informs 25 other potential buyers.

As companies get back to the business basics, managers must recognize the most fundamental of those basics: income comes from customers, not the financial community.

Quality is vital to shaping consumer sentiment, which powers the two-thirds of our economy that is consumer-driven. Quality of productivity is essential for shoring up the economy, especially when business slows down. The value of quality that consumers perceive in products and services exerts an increasingly powerful influence on their spending, especially when money is tight.

Productivity, always a primary driver of prosperity and profitability, is a continuing key to this economic strength. Productivity also particularly relates to the ways in which fundamental business innovation is key to competing and necessary for making technology effective and profitable.

The Internet, almost universally understood as a multipurpose technology, is helping define effectiveness in terms of both product development and new productivity. It confronts companies with demands for innovation that extend far beyond technology. It also confronts companies with basic issues of innovation in regard to making their fiscal discipline as focused as their market development.

Most management leaders understand that the one certainty in business is that the environment will continue changing. They recognize that leadership in this environment requires understanding the characteristics of the initiatives that will support strong earnings growth in turbulent market conditions.

New powers of leadership and management are creating initiatives for meeting these demands in companies that have become pacesetters. These powers will be a strong force in governing the way business operates.

Pacesetter companies are succeeding with a leadership attitude characterized by a firm financial responsibility to customers, investors, employees, and other stakeholders. This attitude focuses simultaneously on the rewards and risks of opportunistic growth, the immense potential of more effective human resources, and the speed of action required to succeed.

The truths of our business environment lead to these three conclusions:

Be quick and flexible: Agility is the key to adapting to changes. Networking and diffusion work better than bureaucracy.

Emphasize and encourage creativity: This ability is more and more important. It is essential in thinking beyond the conventional.

Trust your employees: The people closest to what is happening can lead and improve it most effectively. Allow all employees access to the information that can help them make decisions. Give them the authority to make those decisions.

"In these times when the fast devour the slow, productivity particularly relates to the significance of the ways in which a company can maintain its fundamental business innovation as a key to its competitive leadership."

☐ Try things here and there

☑ **Sustain and systematize**

More and more business managers are coming to recognize a basic principle: There is a fundamental difference between the periodic inspirational creation of big and important management innovative initiatives that provide leadership for a while (until they are no longer a competitive advantage) and the capability of generating an ongoing stream of competitive leadership business innovation through management systems and processes that can sustain continuing growth.

The companies that systematize innovation are stars. The companies moved by spurts of inspiration are comets, flashing up for a short time and then down again as their management competitive strength burns out. In these comet organizations, competitive leadership depends on the personalities of their managers rather than a carefully systematic emphasis.

The discipline that drives innovation in pacesetter companies is built on the experience that major improvements in 21st-century businesses involve a better way to run the business—which, at the same time, also positions a company to find a further better way to run the business.

Even in pacesetter companies, as business circumstances or managers change, the leading-edge competence may die and be buried without an autopsy or it may become a bureaucratic initiative in the hands of a few specialists rather than diffused, encouraged, and supported throughout the company.

Systematizing management innovation in the 21st century is parallel to the systematization of technology and product development in the 20th century, when new product development became a corporate way of thinking and doing, beyond the traditional R&D laboratory or occasional flashes or revelations. New product development was an area of leadership success that differentiated corporate leaders from their competitors. Now, systematizing management innovation is the critical success factor for 21st-century pacesetter companies.

For success and sustained growth, here are three requisites:

Systematize innovation: Learn from the bad experiences of companies that have been good at periodic bursts of innovation but weak in implementing systematic leadership, attitudes, and disciplines for innovation. Benefit from the examples of companies that emphasize continuing and further management innovations.

Develop discipline: Understand that experience shows that major improvements must involve a better way to run the business. Trust that this better way positions a company to continue to find better ways.

Establish systematization of management innovation as an overarching theme: Make it a fundamental way to lead and manage, the guide to corporate action. Promote it as the corporate mindset.

"There is a fundamental difference between periodic inspirational creation of big and important management innovative initiatives that provide leadership for a while ... and competitive business innovation through management systems and processes that can sustain continuing growth."

☐ ~~Keep talking concepts~~

☑ Operationalize concepts

What sets pacesetter companies apart is their effectiveness in the third fundamental change in management. They have systematically operationalized the concept of the 21st-century company that is built on understanding and focusing on value-added intangibles and soft assets at least as much as hard assets. They have transformed this concept from an abstraction, words in executive discussions, into a competitive strength, focusing on results and emphasizing management innovation.

Operationalizing emphasizes measuring these results case by case, which also can contribute to the progressive quantification of intangible factors in terms that can then be combined with the quantification of tangible factors.

General Electric, setting the pace very early, developed its "boundaryless" behavior initiative for focusing the entire company on breaking down the walls of traditional decentralization, which was the heart of the hierarchical concept of the corporation.

Another example of systemic innovation is Walmart. It took the lead in management by integrating the best of traditional merchandising and supplier practices with the best of the new information and other technology initiatives. It has also emphasized face-to-face, multichannel selling of broad ranges of goods and services. It provides integrated support through its Internet supply chain network that connects with a wide range of resources. Reportedly, links to banks may enable the company to pay suppliers as soon as a purchase crosses the bar-code reader at checkout. This technology that improves its suppliers' cash flow enables Walmart to demand discounts from suppliers that can translate into lower prices.

Make your company more effective in this fundamental change in management by doing these three things:

Move from words into action: Operationalize the concept of focusing more on value-added intangibles and soft assets. Turn it into a competitive strength. Emphasize results and management innovation.

Benchmark other companies systematically: Learn from the companies that are ahead of the pack. Study your competitors—and any companies that are improving their operations and management.

Push for major innovation breakthroughs in management: Think about how you would build your company if you started at zero. Implement those breakthroughs aggressively.

"In a study of more than 600 companies with strong total quality management initiatives, the companies that emphasized best practices and benchmarking averaged a 44 percent higher stock price return, 48 percent higher growth in operating income, and 37 percent higher growth in sales."

☑ Lead with heart and head

Implementation of management capital capacity involves the following factors:

- Leadership and management passion, populism, and disciplined responsibility that bring focus to the theme of management capital, underpin the processes for its continuous implementation, and develop the character of the company.

- Creation and continuing development of the environment and framework for involving the creativity, knowledge, skills, and attitudes of all members of the organization in improving results.

- Systematic identification of the major business issues and opportunities confronting top-line growth and bottom-line profitability in terms of creating value for customers, investors, and employees. These issues may be *visible*—related to products, services, and markets—or *invisible*—related to how the company operates, with measurement of related business failure costs.

- Relentless and rigorous development and improvement of the strategy, discipline, and process for solving problems and creating opportunities.
- Digitizing of key business operations and processes as economically appropriate.
- Effective ongoing emphasis on effective execution of all these initiatives to promote competitive leadership.

The result of these factors is that the effectiveness of management capital and the systems and process leadership that underpin it explicitly become one of the new central leading indicators of sustained corporate profitability and growth. Management capital is a key factor by which corporate growth and earnings can be predicted and an important component of economic analysis. It is also a major factor in the focus and meaning of managing with an attitude that will sustain growth in the face of new economic challenges.

Our experience shows that capitalizing management power is driven by a company's leaders and management attitudes that reflect the new economic, human, technological, and global demands for sustaining profitable business growth. These attitudes create this new management model and its organization and implementation. Implementation will, of course, continue to vary according to markets, products and services, personalities, competitive conditions, and other circumstances.

Pursue the following three directions to maximize management capital capacity:

Promote passion, populism, and disciplined responsibility: Use these qualities to develop the character of the company.

Build the right setting: Create the environment and framework for involving the creativity, knowledge, skills, and attitudes throughout the organization to improve results. Continue developing this setting: change is necessary and innovation is key.

Identify issues and opportunities: Make this a systematic responsibility. Find ways to promote top-line growth and bottom-line profitability and create value for customers, investors, and employees.

"In the beginning years of the 21st century, many companies and business leaders have a quality of management that is a new competitive leadership combination of passion, populism, and disciplined responsibility—the basic foundation for capitalizing management power."

☐ ~~Use more management~~

☑ Manage better not more

Pacesetter companies do not consider their strength in terms of the quantity of management of the hierarchical leadership of earlier times, but rather the quality of management, the leadership and networking capability for focusing all resources on sustaining business growth.

The objective is to create constant momentum for establishing and maintaining competitive leadership in all the principal management channels across the company's business value chain. Experience has identified 12 key channels of management capital in pacesetter companies:

1. New product/service development and introduction
2. Marketing
3. Expansion and globalization
4. Total quality for product, process, and service excellence
5. Management measurement

6. Partnership and alliance development
7. Operations
8. Supply management
9. Human resources
10. Integrated business information management
11. Financial operations
12. Asset management

A company's effectiveness in these channels, particularly in its opportunity areas, is key to its competitive strength. That effectiveness depends on competitive leadership in the systems and end-to-end processes, tools, resources, and strategies that create the basic learning framework and motivational strength. That effectiveness also enables the company's leaders to measure results and improve business value.

Management knowledge has become globalized. Companies everywhere are following best practices in management. However, there is an enormous difference in business results among companies.

Knowledge is power—but only when company leaders understand that a culture for sustaining growth is defined primarily by its actions for growth and for systematically identifying and removing obstacles while driving performance in new ways. Quality of leadership must be pervasive throughout the system.

Here are three ways to promote quality of management and leadership:

Focus on quality of management leadership: Emphasize systematic capabilities that establish, align, and integrate your company's strategy, objectives, and measurements with its work processes. Do this in all the key business areas. Make it the foundation of a balanced approach to leadership.

Promote competitive leadership in all the principal management channels: Strengthen your company's business value chain through better management, not more. Build your competitive advantage through becoming more effective, particularly in those channels in your company's opportunity areas.

Enable and encourage each member of the organization to provide superior performance: Use processes, tools, and strategies that help all people, individually and in teams, to think, learn, act, and make decisions about how to improve value for customers and, consequently, for investors.

"The key point is this: the attitude, process, and management capital disciplines create the structure and organization for this quality-of-management emphasis—not vice versa."

☐ ~~Hold on to traditions~~

☑ Create the future

Pacesetting companies discard management doctrines that no longer work, like these:

Good management means getting ideas from the boss to the workers. Good management means maximizing on the knowledge, skills, and attitudes of all employees to make improvements throughout the organization.

Corporate and management change must be incremental. Make improvements on a broad front, developing understanding and support throughout the organization. Establish a prioritization sequence to schedule improvements more time-efficiently.

Deliver products and services quicker and cheaper, sell hard, and provide a service safety net for customer problems. Customer expectations have changed dramatically, so this approach costs a lot in lost customers and fixes. Competitive leaders make better products and offer better services.

The Internet is primarily a technology. It's much more. It's a business model with processes for anticipating customer behaviors, recognizing market changes, and increasing sales. It's an ecosystem connecting a company externally with suppliers and customers and internally through a network among employees.

Emphasizing traditional cost accounting is the primary way to reduce costs and focus improvement. You can miss key opportunities and unnecessary costs, because traditional cost measurement can neglect processes that are increasingly important areas for improvement.

Focusing on internal improvement generates the earliest and best results. This approach can divert attention from customers and employees and from identifying and building on strengths for understanding and serving customers. Take a multidimensional integrated approach.

Organization decentralization is invariably good in itself. Decentralization must be carefully balanced and evaluated or huge problems arise in allocating financial capital, marketing, and operating costs. Make company size a strength through suitable integration of common resources that benefit all business units.

HR enhancement programs can succeed through extensive motivational displays and executive speeches. For these programs to succeed, operating practices must enable employees to use whatever knowledge and skills the programs are promoting.

Executive leadership is essential only in being competitive with products and services. Executives must also lead another competition—between the company's processes and patterns and the processes and patterns of its competitors.

You can buy improvement leadership results through an emphasis on financial capital. You must also manage smarter by integrating human, physical, and financial factors.

Manage smarter:

Exorcise management doctrines that no longer apply: Rid the company of management doctrines that have become irrelevant and ineffective, working against profitability and growth.

Make sure that business leadership initiatives are paying off: Don't keep them for sentimental reasons.

Examine all doctrines and initiatives carefully before trying any: Don't play follow the leader—unless it can make you a leader.

"Failed acquisitions, overleveraged mergers, massive reduction of human resources, and overinvestment in capacity far in excess of market potential are some outcomes of making financial capital the basis and center point for growth and profitability."

☐ ~~Keep power at the top~~

☑ Network responsibility

A company's character defines its culture. Employees understand it, astute investors consider it an important factor in their investment decisions, and experienced customers can sense it when making buying decisions. That character strengthens or weakens as the company acts or only reacts to demands of the business world. The speed and effectiveness with which it acts depend on how well the people throughout the company are systematically connected with those demands so that they can execute and implement actions quickly and strongly.

Whether a company is large or small, its speed and effectiveness depend on the networking and diffusion of responsibility, understanding, commitment, and execution and implementation throughout the organization to pace and guide its business growth and on the attitude that "we will all work together." Pacesetter companies depend on their management capital emphasis as the foundation guidelines for integrating networking, diffusion, and attitude throughout the organization.

What distinguishes pacesetter companies is their emphasis on the competitive power that results from making management innovation systematic while recognizing and preserving the competitive strength of its fundamental and unique competitive advantage "signature" capabilities developed over time.

Leaders of pacesetter companies lead with a fundamentally new competitive combination of passion, populism, and disciplined responsibility that is reflected in a bias for action. They make management innovation systematic and a business "way of life."

Continuous systematic management innovation is not only a significant competitive strength for pacesetter companies but also for companies whose business results have been less continuous and are supported much less by signature capabilities.

Network responsibility and power throughout your company:

Build on innovation: Maintain your competitive and profitability advantage by systematizing innovation. Enable people throughout your organization to make improvements. Make innovation and improvement part of your "signature" capabilities.

Sustain and accelerate profitability and growth through focusing on the key performance results: Focus on market leadership, operating costs, human resource effectiveness, organization responsiveness, close and constructive relationships with business partners, and rigorous recognition of responsibilities—to the public, investors, and employees and for the environment and safety.

Pursue "temporary monopoly power": Keep in mind that in the new economy "the only incentive to produce anything is the possession of temporary monopoly power ..., so the constant pursuit of that temporary monopoly power becomes the central driving thrust of the new economy." Push to innovate quickly and grab the largest possible market ... and then keep pushing to innovate.

"A company's character is the collective result of its actions—and certainly the actions of its management."

☐ ~~Work independently~~

☑ **Collaborate strategically**

A major characteristic of the 21st-century business environment is that many companies are becoming more competitive through allying with companies that provide necessary capabilities—even though a high proportion of such alliances have not worked out.

Acquisitions require fundamental changes in control and ownership. Mergers place correspondingly enormous management capital demands on the timely focusing of resources to achieve the business objectives.

Other forms of business relationships are very different from the pattern of trade mergers and acquisitions. The objective of creating strategic alliances is to develop forms of cooperation with organizations that provide competitive capabilities. These relationships require forms of integration that are completely different from management based on ownership and control.

Similar developments have been taking place through many other forms of alliances, such as when a larger company acquires a minority stake in a small company. This is a growing trend, particularly in big companies that buy significant quantities of equipment from smaller companies. Similar trends are occurring in research and marketing agreements that involve cooperation but certainly not control and ownership, particularly in areas of development in which a few years ago a major company would instead have made an acquisition.

An equally important trend is the development of relationships for particular purposes between companies that are otherwise strong competitors in their major markets.

These trends are showing that single, long-term business management models do not fit every situation for a company. The leadership and management demands for these alliance models differ greatly from those for the model based on the hierarchy of ownership and control rather than on networking it. The effectiveness of a company's management-capital theme and attitude becomes even more important for achieving the intended integration and confluence.

Improve your competitive strength by collaborating smart with other organizations:

Form strategic alliances: Increase your capability through allying with organizations that provide capabilities that complement yours.

Consider investing in other organizations: Examine the potential benefits of acquiring a minority stake in a supplier, for example.

Explore the value of other business relationships: Success does not always depend on beating your competitors. Remember that even competitors can collaborate.

"In the 21st century the old business concept that single, long-term business management models should fit all situations for a company is no longer the pattern (if, in fact, it ever really was)."

☑ Compete using technology

Information, software, communications, and Internet technologies offer great potential for creating major new business opportunities. They form the foundation not only for creating major new products but also for developing and producing existing products more effectively.

Being a leader is the key to achieving the important business rewards in market share and profitability. The objective is to be number one or number two, because success begets success.

This is particularly evident in e-business and e-commerce. The strong first-mover companies focus on rigorous maintenance of their processes for availability of both the best selection of products and the best customer traffic. Most markets can support only two or three leaders and brands.

The pressures in this new competitive landscape have created new demands throughout the business value chain of companies both large and small. These changes all contribute to gradually but significantly changing customer expectations, employee attitudes, international growth, and cost trends.

These nine areas offer such opportunities for improving competitive position:

1. global expansion
2. time cycle compression
3. customer satisfaction
4. managing information technology
5. product and service innovation
6. supply management
7. quality
8. asset monetization
9. environmental demands and risk management

A tenth major opportunity is the Internet. It is a key enabler for companies that are developing their management capital and implementing systematic and continuing management innovation. It is also a growing force for companies that are trying to improve the use of their total resources in order to accelerate business results.

Five broad areas have proved to be particularly important for successful and continuing digitized management innovation:

1. manufacturing and production
2. marketing and sales
3. supply
4. malls and exchanges

5. product development networks for customers, dealers, and user-participants

Keep in mind these three points when using technology:

Lead with your technology: Remember that the corporate differentiator lies in what a company can do with technology, not solely in being the first with innovative technology. Be clearly and inspirationally directed by your customers and markets. Quickly integrate your technology innovations throughout your business structure.

Find opportunities: Explore particularly the possibilities in the nine areas listed above.

Recognize that the Internet is open to all: Emphasize, when developing Internet-related management innovation initiatives, that your unique competitive strength lies in how you manage, lead, and implement the initiative and particularly how effectively you develop and install the processes that are the foundation for improving performance. Focus on the five eras listed above.

"Technology generates its full power only when the effectiveness of a company's product technology capability is matched by the effectiveness of its business leadership capability: its management innovations and its constancy of management capital."

☐ ~~Focus on fighting fires~~

☑ Find and fix disconnects

The forces of the changing marketplace and technology, among other factors, can result in significant business disconnects.

They develop when it is assumed that leadership and management practices that worked well in the past will continue to work well. This assumption is especially problematic because some of these carryover leadership and management practices are still firmly embedded in the way some companies work. Management channels may grow out of touch with these changing business requirements unless there is strong leadership.

Carryover business issues arise when periods of long economic expansion are followed by major economic change. This creates enormous business challenges for companies positioning themselves to seize these new opportunities.

Companies are caught between the strong upward pressure on costs created by the increases companies continue to face and the severe downward pressure on price created by market changes. In some companies this can progressively create what we call "backward creep" in performance. This backward creep is gradually reflected in technology, customer satisfaction performance, employee attitudes, and cost trends. It can happen even if it seems that a company's business practices may be having good results.

Disconnects create a "hidden organization." Employees are diverted from their goals because they must continually try to patch together disconnects or work their way through them. Managers are less effective because of disconnects.

The company's leaders must give key areas "a business physical"—a regular check-up. They need to understand how extensive and fundamental their management innovation must be to help employees throughout the company achieve the necessary improvement results.

Companies now recognize that they can reap an enormous profitability and growth advantage by focusing on reconnecting these disconnects. Continuous management improvement is a basic key.

Create and maintain the management capital attitude and emphasis that create and maintain competitive strength:

Manage with passion: Recognize that the pursuit of excellence is the most powerful emotional motivator in any organization. Use passion to relentlessly drive effective improvement through strong and consistent management of the organization's balanced and integrated actions.

Manage through populism: Populism emphasizes the commitment, knowledge, and skill of all the members of the organization. Populism enables by allowing the freedom to innovate, to solve problems cooperatively, and to use teamwork.

Manage with disciplined responsibility: Provide the systems, processes, tools, resources, and strategies that help and encourage all members of the organization to think, act, and make decisions about how to provide superior performance.

"It is hazardous to assume that leadership and management practices that worked well in the past will be similarly effective in the very different economy of the next several years, especially considering the enormous technological developments that have accompanied this change."

☐ Pay costs of doing business

☑ End costs of failure

A basic key in creating new business opportunity is to increase product and service value for customers while simultaneously eliminating obstacles. This means measuring disconnects and backward creep as costs of failures and lost opportunities and working to reduce those costs.

Customer expectations, employee attitudes, technology shifts, international growth, and cost trends change quickly. Companies that seem to be doing well in terms of growth and profits can become increasingly distanced from recognizing, evaluating, and improving the fundamental drivers of their performance.

The disconnects and the management capital deficiencies that are a primary cause of those disconnects can diminish a company's capacity for sustaining profitable growth. Frequently financial analysts and cost accountants who focus on hard assets are unable to identify the root causes of those costs and quantify them.

One way is to measure the quality costs of ensuring complete customer satisfaction with the company's products and services as a percentage of sales revenue. Costs measured in these terms have four components:

1. **External failure costs**—including costs generated by the unsatisfactory performance of products and services and related tasks

2. **Internal failure costs**—including costs generated within the company network by this unsatisfactory performance

3. **Appraisal**—including costs associated with key systems, processes, and Internet functions that provide controls to ensure customer satisfaction

4. **Prevention**—including costs associated with initiatives for preventing disconnects and backward creep that can affect customer satisfaction

Pacesetter companies have the management capital and capacities to connect increasing customer value and removing obstacles. Those capacities are strategized and planned and then networked and diffused throughout the organization, with a systems and process effectiveness that enables and encourages every person—individually and in teams—to rapidly and consistently think, act, decide on, and integrate solutions. An emphasis on being a systematic learning organization is a crucial part of a character and culture for sustaining and extending profitable growth.

Reduce or eliminate costs of failures and lost opportunities by improving management thinking:

Promote rigorous system process methodology: Emphasize long-term detailed system implementation of initiatives and continuous improvement led by senior managers.

Define company results in terms of your customers: Work to deliver products and services with higher customer value quicker and cheaper.

Enable and empower your employees: Provide appropriate training consistent with systems. Stress continuous learning. Focus on making your customers happy. Make improvement a major factor in recognition and rewards.

"Measuring the disconnects as failure costs and lost opportunity costs and integrating continuous improvement through a rigorous increase in systems effectiveness are a central part of the leadership attitude of opportunistically driven pacesetting companies."

☐ ~~Go your own way~~

☑ **Lead with the best**

Whatever its products or services, fundamental to what a company is really developing, producing, and marketing is the intellectual content, the human resources-motivated competence, and the other soft-asset capabilities that go into these products and services.

How effectively a company manages these capabilities to provide the value of a completely satisfactory customer experience that will develop loyalty and repeat business is what determines its ability to make the large and small moves that now drive competitive leadership.

Four primary business characteristics stand out in the management capital attitude and emphasis of companies that are doing this.

1. Understanding, respecting, and responding to customers is critical. Pacesetter companies emphasize leadership that responds to the fundamental shift in customer expectations that has been driven by the explosion of demand for greater purchase value. They understand that there is no substitute for direct contact with their customers in the forms that best fit the situation.

2. Being a leader requires the extension of leadership throughout the organization. Pacesetter companies emphasize prudent, effective, open, responsible action and disclosure that take into account the business realities of economic fluctuations and up-and-down cycles. They pay attention to short- and long-term performance because customers, investors, and others focus on both and because the single toughest job for management is to build forward momentum—and if it slips it may be impossible to recover.

3. A company should be continuously improving and informing customers of the improvements. Pacesetter companies use consistent improvement to promotional advantage. When customers think about products and services, they also think about the company's reputation.

4. Continuous improvement requires specific objectives, with a timetable, structure, and support to meet those objectives and with the expectation of excellence in implementing changes. Pacesetter companies recognize that their culture for improvement is far more than a philosophy supported by incremental improvement, a problematic patchwork of projects.

Lead by learning from the best practices of pace-setter companies:

Talk with your customers: Ask them what they think. Supplement the results of market research. Make direct contact with your customers a rigorous discipline, since it can be very difficult to do in the face of time pressures.

Concentrate on being better and getting credit for it: Use consistent improvement to sell your company. Promote it as strongly as you promote your products and services.

Structure continuous improvement: Set specific objectives. Create a timetable. Develop a structure and support. Lead implementation and execution of your plans.

"Judgment and intellect have increasingly become the powerhouse of business and organizational results when they are effectively led, inspired, managed, networked, and diffused by means of the empowerment of end-to-end systems and processes in key management capital channels."

☐ ~~Improve however, whenever~~

☑ Cultivate best practices

A fundamental factor in business leadership is to systematically establish best practices and the knowledge, skills, learning steps, and attitudes that create and implement these practices, with these objectives:

- What works well anywhere in the organization becomes quickly available everywhere in the organization.
- Size is used as a strength rather than allowed to become a weakness as the company grows.
- Organizational wisdom becomes consolidated in guidelines for aligned actions throughout the organization.

These best practices integrate both tangible and intangible competitive strengths. These practices are developed and used in all key areas, leveraged throughout the organization in any form that makes them immediately available and easy to use for every member—intranet, Internet, audiovisual, process documentation, and so on.

Pacesetter companies develop, manage, and maintain the information management systems that provide the process foundation for the creation of best practices. This emphasis on *systematic management of information integration* differs fundamentally from a fascination with information technology in and of itself. It enables a company to achieve and sustain superior performance through information process support of all operations. Without this systematic information management and ongoing discipline, the use of best practices would be incremental, not enough for best practice competitive strength.

Competitors can comparison shop, engineer, and readily track products and services. It is far more difficult for them to determine how the company is managing to work more effectively than its competitors. This is an enormous competitive advantage in a time when a technology or a product or service application can spread within a few weeks throughout companies around the world that are targeting the same customers. Even if its know-how emerges, the company is already involved in developing other competitive edges, operating on the principle that a better way to compete means positioning the company for a further better way to compete.

Cultivate best practices in the following ways:

Take competitive advantage of your best practices: Develop and use them in all key areas. Make your best practices immediately available and easy to use.

Review all decisions concerning products or services: Discuss the benefits of remaining in the market to retain customer relationships. Consider whether to discontinue the product or service. Do not hesitate to "mess with success."

Do information management, not just information technology: Develop a competitive edge by networking and diffusing support throughout the company infrastructure and e-frastructure. Integrate, maintain, and continually upgrade the information process support of all operations.

"The best practices component of a company's management capital includes the knowledge, skills, learning steps, and attitudes that create and implement these practices throughout the company."

☐ ~~Manage to survive~~

☑ **Lead competitively**

Business leaders must lead and manage success-fully, systematically, and opportunistically for results that sustain profitability and growth in terms that confirm their company's character and combine its visible and invisible competitive strengths.

This means establishing overarching themes for capitalizing their management power to fit their particular requirements, personality, and customer and business demands.

There are four dimensions to leading competitively.

1. A new, more powerful emphasis on customer value for marketing and sales strength, including product and service development. Customers are becoming better informed and more demanding. Companies must fully meet the demands and expectations of their customers.

That means satisfying customers with their products and services and with how they are presented, sold, serviced, and supported. Quality is what the customers think it is. And it must be managed and measured in these terms. Moreover, it is a constantly changing target that must be tracked continually in a brutally competitive marketplace. Understanding customer value and providing it ensure competitive marketing and sales strength.

2. Operating cost leadership for the company's economic strength. A company must rigorously make reducing production costs an integral part of day-by-day leadership and management. This means consistently and systematically eliminating business failure costs, disconnects, and backward creep in performance.

3. Management innovation and total resource use for competitive business improvement. The emphasis here is on systematizing management innovation to improve leadership and management in ways that position the company for further improvement. Pacesetter companies measure the results in clear financial terms.

4. Empowering a company culture of superior performance. Pacesetter companies focus using the passion, populism, and disciplined responsibility of their leaders to generate energy for integrating, networking, and channeling all company resources to sustain and accelerate profitability and growth throughout the key management capital channels.

Here are three ways to lead competitively:

Understand quality: Accept that it means whatever the customer says and believes that it means—no more, no less. Keep tracking what quality means to your customers and how they feel about what you're offering.

Recognize the meaning of major business improvement: Understand that it means a better way to run the company that also positions it for further improvement. Measure the results in clear financial terms.

Develop a culture of excellence: Channel the passion, populism, and disciplined responsibility of company leaders to generate energy throughout the organization. Integrate, network, and deploy all resources throughout the key management capital channels.

"The requirement is for leading and managing successfully, systematically, and opportunistically. The objectives are results that sustain and accelerate profitability and growth in terms that confirm a company's character and bring together its visible and invisible strengths for competitive leadership."

☐ Focus on the bottom line

☑ Lead your value chain

Seven characteristics distinguish competitive leadership.

1. Personal senior leadership of the quality-of-management process. Senior managers are continually involved in creating and maintaining the company's quality-of-management process. They lead with a clear vision for improvement.

2. Structure to capitalize management strength and best use of total resources. Pacesetter leaders form structures that effectively and productively network and diffuse the company's full capabilities and integrate visible and invisible competitive strengths within the framework of strategic planning, business planning, annual operating plans, alignment of business objectives, and performance management.

3. Set clear, firm goals, involving employees in developing and implementing them. Pacesetter leaders develop realistic stretch goals according to the company's character, culture, and quality of management leadership. They develop those goals through input from the employees who are closest to the work and the customers.

4. Emphasize executing, innovating, reducing distance, and eliminating disconnects and failure costs. Leaders take action. They work to eliminate disconnects and corresponding failure costs. They promote management innovation in all key value-creating competitive areas. They close the distances between management and employees and between employees and customers.

5. Create an environment of positive attitude, opportunistic involvement, and empowerment. Pacesetting leaders recognize that employees often oppose change but learn to accept it when their knowledge, skills, and attitudes become deeply involved in developing and implementing this change. They create an environment of trust, openness, and honest communication to encourage the development of "individual job entrepreneurs," providing knowledge, training, and opportunities.

6. Emphasis on short-term as well as long-term goals. Leaders know that there is no long term without the short term. They know that small successes lead to great successes, motivate employees, and build momentum.

7. Emphasis on partnerships and alliances throughout the value chain. Pacesetting leaders establish continuously better relationships with organizations that are important to the company. They appreciate companies that are flexible and able and willing to help in critical situations.

Lead competitively throughout your value chain:

Focus on improvement: Express excellence in your vision. Show confidence in your employees. Remember that the pursuit of excellence is the most powerful emotional motivator.

Be smart about making changes: Create a positive attitude and opportunistic involvement, using the company vision as a focus. Emphasize effective and ongoing communication. Plan and then move quickly.

Develop your value chain: Take advantage of full-service supply concepts. Build partnerships and alliances. Consider cooperating with your competitors.

"A leadership characteristic that defines management excellence is the ability to establish better and more productive relationships, not only with suppliers but also with the other organizations that are important to the success and growth of a company. Demanding times require such new and more effective economic partnerships and alliances."

☐ ~~Manage the old way~~

☑ **Manage by the new model**

There are two fundamental ways to compete.

The first is to effectively and efficiently lead the *visible* value creation competitive strength of the company. This involves managing in terms of selling more products and services. This effectiveness and efficiency are measured by sales and market scorecard criteria that are widely recognized, universally available, and often rigorously benchmarked. This approach to competition is what has traditionally been meant by "competitive leadership."

Management leadership of value-creating visible competition is a basic condition for success. It tracks the direct source of revenues. It is the in-line operation of running the business to generate these revenues.

However, this is an era of changing market expectations, fickle customer tastes, explosive commoditization of products and services, and exponentially better quality, cost, and delivery improvements. Now companies need to do more to compete.

The second way is *invisible* value creation competitive strength. This is leadership in terms of being better, not just more profitable. It is how an organization thinks, learns, decides, and—most important—acts. It is managing the competitive strength that derives from the way an organization performs far better than its competitors in recruiting, staffing, and motivating, as well as in developing, selling, financing, and maintaining its products and services—with far lower business failure costs.

Pacesetter companies excel in integrating the management of their visible and invisible value-creating competitive strengths. They have leaders with the skill, know-how, and commitment to manage by this new model.

This approach fundamentally changes the line-and-staff model of traditional management, in which running the business and improving the business are separate channels. Instead, these functions are integrated bases for achieving business results.

As companies flattened organizationally in the last decade, the traditional corporate staff often disappeared. Yet the improvement processes have become progressively more important. This model builds on that new reality.

Manage your company by the new model:

Don't depend on visible value-creation competitive strength: Don't emphasize traditional measures of success. Balance management of visible value-creation competition with management of invisible value-creation competition.

Develop and exercise leadership in managing invisible value-creation competitive strength: Improve the way your people think and act. Recruit better and treat your employees better. Be a better place to work than your competitors.

Utilize staff functions effectively: Make staff functions a further way to generate business results. Integrate *running* the business and *improving* the business.

"What sets the character of pacesetter companies apart is the emphasis those companies place on making management innovation systematic and a business way of life."

"A management committed to innovation provides an enormous business strength for leadership in systematically—rather than incrementally—dealing with today's improvement imperative."

"Quality-of-management leadership creates the power of an environment of trust, openness, and honest communication to encouage the development of what we have described as 'individual job entrepreneurs.'"

"A company's character defines its culture. Employees understand it (even if they cannot always articulate it), astute investors try to employ it as an important factor in their investment decisions, and experienced customers can sense it when they make repeat buying decisions."

The McGraw-Hill Mighty Manager's Handbooks

The Powell Principles

by Oren Harari (0-07-144490-4)

Details two dozen mission- and people-based leadership skills that have guided Colin Powell through his nearly half-century of service to the United States.

Provides a straight-to-the-point guide that any leader in any arena can follow for unmitigated success.

How Buffett Does It

by James Pardoe (0-07-144912-4)

Expands on 24 primary ideas Warren Buffett has followed from day one.

Reveals Buffett's stubborn adherence to the time-honored fundamentals of value investing.

The Lombardi Rules

by Vince Lombardi, Jr. (0-07-144489-0)

Presents more than two dozen of the tenets and guidelines Lombardi used to drive him and those around him to unprecedented levels of success.

Packed with proven insights and techniques that are especially valuable in today's turbulent business world.

The Welch Way

by Jeffrey A. Krames (0-07-142953-0)

Draws on the career of Jack Welch to explain how workers can follow his proven model.

Shows how to reach new heights in today's wide-open, idea-driven workplace.

The Ghosn Factor

by Miguel Rivas-Micoud (0-07-148595-3)

Examines the life, works, and words of Carlos Ghosn, CEO of *Nissan* and *Renault.*

Provides 24 succinct lessons that managers can immediately apply.

How to Motivate Every Employee

by Anne Bruce (0-07-146330-5)

Provides strategies for infusing your employees with a passion for the work they do.

Packed with techniques, tips, and suggestions that are proven to motivate in all industries and environments.

The New Manager's Handbook

by Morey Stettner (0-07-146332-1)

Gives tips for teaming with your employees to achieve extraordinary goals.

Outlines field-proven techniques to succeed and win the respect of both your employees and your supervisors.

The Sales Success Handbook

by Linda Richardson (0-07-146331-3)

> Shows how to sell customers—not by what you tell them, but by how well you listen to what they have to say.

> Explains how to persuasively position the value you bring to meet the customer's business needs.

How to Plan and Execute Strategy

by Wallace Stettinius, D. Robley Wood, Jr., Jacqueline L. Doyle, and John L. Colley, Jr. (0-07-148437-X)

> Provides 24 practical steps for devising, implementing, and managing market-defining, growth-driving strategies.

> Outlines a field-proven framework that can be followed to strengthen your company's competitive edge.

How to Manage Performance

by Robert Bacal (0-07-148439-8)

> Provides goal-focused, common-sense techniques to stimulate employee productivity in any environment.

> Details how to align employee goals and set performance incentives.

Managing in Times of Change

by Michael D. Maginn (0-07-148436-1)

> Helps you to understand and explain the benefits of change, while flourishing within the new environment.

> Provides straight talk and actionable advice for teams, managers, and individuals.

About the Authors

Armand V. Feigenbaum, Ph.D. is the recipient of the National Medal of Technology and Innovation for 2007, America's highest innovation and technology award. He is the originator of Total Quality Control, which was conceived while he was earning his doctoral degree from MIT.

He is the recipient of numerous honors from major bodies and associations around the world. Dr. Feigenbaum is the president and CEO of the international systems engineering company, General Systems, Inc., which develops and installs management systems that accelerate profitability and growth for major manufacturing, technology, and service companies in the United States, as well as throughout North and South America, Europe, and Asia.

Donald S. Feigenbaum, Sc.D. is chief operating officer and executive vice president of General Systems, Inc. Dr. Feigenbaum is an acknowledged world leader in systems management and engineering practices that have provided favorable results in implementing the competitive business strengths and profitability of principal manufacturing, technology, and service companies. Dr. Feigenbaum has published numerous influential works in systems management that are seminal influences on management practices for accelerating profitability and growth in organizations throughout the world.

For information about the authors or the application of Management Innovation™, visit **www.managementcapital.com**.